Story of a Storm

Mick Manning
and Brita Granström

W
FRANKLIN WATTS
LONDON·SYDNEY

For Kristina Granström
with love

Many thanks to the Fairbairn family
and their beautiful heavy horses.

First published in 2001
by Franklin Watts,
96 Leonard Street,
London EC2A 4XD

Franklin Watts Australia
56 O'Riordan Street
Alexandria
NSW 2015

The illustrations in this book have been drawn
by both Mick and Brita

Text and illustrations © 2001 Mick Manning
and Brita Granström
Series editor: Rachel Cooke
Art director: Jonathan Hair

Printed in Hong Kong, China
A CIP catalogue record is available from
the British Library.
Dewey Classification 551.55
ISBN 0 7496 4180 0

Contents

Dark clouds

Dark clouds were chasing each other over the mountains . . .

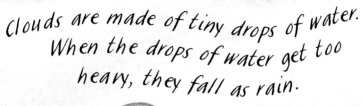

Clouds are made of tiny drops of water.
When the drops of water get too
heavy, they fall as rain.

7

The wind began to blow . . .

Winds are caused by air
moving around the earth.

Winds can be gentle breezes
or sometimes stormy gales.

9

It's raining

Then came the first
spots of rain . . .
A storm was
on its way!

Rain can be a light drizzle.
A short spell of rain is called a shower.

When there's a real downpour,
we say it's raining cats and dogs.

11

It began to pour down.

You can study the weather by measuring rainfall and wind speeds.

13

The wind grew stronger -
lashing the rain against
fur and skin!

14

Lightning strikes tall pointed shapes, so never shelter under a tree in a storm. Try to get indoors or inside a car.

If you are stuck outside, lie down until the storm passes.

15

The Storm

CRASH! BANG! KERBAM!
Thunder and lightning
ripped across the sky . . .

16

Lightning is a huge electric shock which passes between clouds and the ground. Thunder is the bang caused by the electricity exploding.

It was safe and dry inside
the barn. Outside, the storm
rampaged like an angry giant.

18

In the past, people thought zig-zags of lightning were thunderbolts thrown from the sky by angry gods.

Afterwards

After lunch, the storm died down. What a mess!

Storms can do serious damage.
Strong winds can blow down trees, and
heavy rain causes floods. Twisting tornadoes
can even throw cars into the air.

21

The thunder still grumbled in the distance. Then there was a rainbow!

Rainbows are caused by sunlight shining

through the tiny drops of water in the air.

23

And there,
under the
rainbow, lay
a newborn foal!

24

Weather is always changing, moving around the earth. A storm passes over and then the sun comes out again.

We called him 'Thunderbolt'.

We would always remember
the storm.

Be a storm watcher!

Keep a record of the weather every day in a notebook.

Thunder countdown
Record how close a thunderstorm comes to you. After a lightning flash, count until you hear the thunder. The less you count, the nearer the storm.

Weather forecasts
Make a note of the weather forecasts on TV. Then note what the weather was *really* like. Was the forecast right?

Rainfall record

Keep a track of rainfall by measuring how much water collects in a container each day. Write that down, too.

Weather sayings

Collect weather sayings in your notebook and check to see if they are right. Do you know this one? Do you think it's true?

Red sky at night, shepherd's delight.

Red sky in the morning, sailor's warning.

Storm words and index

breeze - a light wind. Page 9

clouds - millions of tiny drops of water that come together in the sky. Clouds can be lots of different shapes - from white and fluffy to dark and heavy. Pages 6, 7

electricity - a type of energy which is made naturally in some storm clouds. This type of electricity is called static electricity. Tiny amounts of static electricity in your clothes sometimes give you a little electric shock. Page 17

gale - a very strong wind. Page 9

lightning - the flash of light made when electricity jumps between storm clouds and the ground. Pages 15, 16, 17, 19

rain - water falling from the sky. Pages 10, 11, 13, 14

rainbow - the bow of coloured light that is formed by sunlight shining through raindrops. Pages 22, 23, 24

thunder - the noise made in a storm by electricity exploding. Pages 16, 17, 22

thunderbolt - another name for a lightning flash. Page 19

tornado - a whirling, twisting funnel of wind. Dust, plants and sometimes even cars and houses are sucked up by the tornado as it moves around. Page 21

wind - moving air. Pages 8, 9, 13, 14